# How to find Clients as a Virtual Assistant

I0490879

# Introduction to the world of virtual assistance

In today's fast-paced world, where businesses and individuals need to keep up with the ever-changing technology landscape, virtual assistance has emerged as a critical service that offers an efficient and effective solution to many challenges. The world of virtual assistance is vast, and it offers a plethora of opportunities for individuals looking to start their own business or work from home.

Virtual assistance refers to the provision of administrative, technical, or creative assistance to businesses or individuals remotely. The virtual assistant (VA) can work from anywhere, as long as they have access to the internet and the necessary tools to complete the work.

The concept of virtual assistance has been around for several years, but it has gained significant traction in recent times. As more businesses and individuals seek to outsource their work, virtual assistants have become a vital part of their operations. Virtual assistants can offer a wide range of services, including administrative support, social media management, bookkeeping, web design, and many others.

One of the most significant advantages of virtual assistance is that it allows businesses and individuals to access a pool of talented professionals from around the world. Virtual assistants come from different backgrounds and have various skillsets, making it easy for businesses and individuals to find the right person for the job.

Starting a career in virtual assistance requires dedication, commitment, and a willingness to learn. You need to have the necessary skills to deliver quality work, and you must be able to manage your time efficiently. However, the benefits of working as a virtual assistant are enormous. You get to set your own hours, work from home, and have the freedom to choose the type of work you want to do.

The virtual assistance industry is constantly evolving, and it offers a lot of opportunities for growth and development. As you gain more experience and expand your skillset, you can take on more complex tasks and work with bigger clients. You can also increase your earning potential by specializing in a particular niche.

In conclusion, the world of virtual assistance offers a wealth of opportunities for individuals looking to start their own business or work from home. With the right skills, dedication, and commitment, you can build a successful career as a virtual assistant. The virtual assistance industry is an exciting and dynamic field that offers endless possibilities for growth and development.

# The importance of finding Clients for a virtual assistant

As a virtual assistant, finding clients is essential for the growth and sustainability of your business. Without clients, you will not have any income, and your business will not be able to survive. Therefore, it is critical to understand the importance of finding clients and developing strategies to attract them to your business.

The first step in finding clients is to define your niche and target market. You need to identify the types of services you want to offer and the specific group of people or businesses that require those services. By identifying your niche and target market, you can tailor your marketing efforts to reach the right people, and you can position yourself as an expert in your field.

One of the most significant benefits of finding clients is that it allows you to build a steady stream of income. As you attract more clients, you will have a consistent flow of work, which will enable you to plan and manage your workload more effectively. You can also increase your earning potential by offering additional services or by upselling to your existing clients.

Finding clients also allows you to build long-term relationships with them. As you work with your clients, you will get to know their needs and requirements, which will enable you to deliver better services. By building trust and credibility with your clients, you can increase the likelihood of repeat business and referrals.

In addition, finding clients allows you to expand your network and build your reputation. By delivering quality work and providing exceptional customer service, you can establish yourself as a reputable virtual assistant. This can lead to more opportunities for work, as well as potential partnerships and collaborations with other professionals in your field.

Perhaps the most emotional aspect of finding clients is the sense of fulfillment that comes with helping others achieve their goals. As a virtual assistant, you have the opportunity to make a significant impact on the lives of your clients by providing them with the support they need to succeed. Whether it is helping them grow their business, manage their workload, or achieve a work-life balance, you can take pride in knowing that you are making a difference in their lives.

In conclusion, finding clients is essential for the success of your virtual assistant business. By identifying your niche and target market, delivering quality work, providing exceptional customer service, and building long-term relationships with your clients, you can build a successful and sustainable business. The emotional reward of helping others achieve their goals is an added benefit that makes the journey of finding clients all the more fulfilling.

# Defining Your Niche and Target Market

One of the most critical steps in building a successful virtual assistant business is defining your niche and target market. Your niche is the area in which you specialize, and your target market is the group of people or businesses that you want to work with. By identifying your niche and target market, you can tailor your services to meet their needs and position yourself as an expert in your field.

The first step in defining your niche is to identify your skills and strengths. What are you good at? What skills do you have that can be leveraged in your virtual assistant business? Once you have identified your skills and strengths, you can start to narrow down your niche.

Next, you need to research the market to see what services are in demand. Look for areas where there is a gap in the market, or where you can offer a unique value proposition. By focusing on a niche that is in demand, you can increase your chances of finding clients and building a successful business.

It is also important to consider your passions and interests when defining your niche. If you are passionate about a particular industry or topic, you are more likely to enjoy the work and deliver better results. For example, if you are passionate about social media, you can specialize in social media management for businesses.

Once you have defined your niche, you need to identify your target market. Your target market is the group of people or businesses that require your services. It is essential to understand their needs, challenges, and pain points, so you can tailor your services to meet their specific requirements.

When identifying your target market, you should consider factors such as demographics, industry, location, and budget. For example, if you specialize in bookkeeping, your target market may be small business owners in a particular industry or location.

Defining your niche and target market has several benefits. First, it allows you to position yourself as an expert in your field, which can help you attract more clients. Second, it enables you to tailor your services to meet the specific needs of your target market, which can lead to higher customer satisfaction. Third, it can help you differentiate yourself from your competitors, which can give you a competitive advantage.

In conclusion, defining your niche and target market is a critical step in building a successful virtual assistant business. By identifying your skills, researching the market, considering your passions and interests, and understanding your target market's needs, you can position yourself as an expert in your field and attract more clients. The emotional reward of working with clients who appreciate your expertise and value your services is an added benefit that makes defining your niche and target market all the more fulfilling.

# Understanding Your Ideal Customer

In order to build a successful virtual assistant business, it is essential to understand your ideal customer. Your ideal customer is the person or business that is the best fit for your services. By understanding your ideal customer, you can tailor your marketing efforts to reach them and position yourself as the perfect solution to their needs.

The first step in understanding your ideal customer is to identify their demographics. Demographics include factors such as age, gender, income, education, and location. By identifying your ideal customer's demographics, you can tailor your marketing efforts to reach the right people.

Next, you need to understand your ideal customer's psychographics. Psychographics include factors such as values, beliefs, interests, and lifestyle. By understanding your ideal customer's psychographics, you can create marketing messages that resonate with them and position yourself as the perfect solution to their needs.

It is also important to understand your ideal customer's pain points and challenges. What are their biggest frustrations? What are the challenges they face in their daily lives or in their business? By understanding your ideal customer's pain points and challenges, you can position yourself as the solution to their problems.

Another important factor to consider when understanding your ideal customer is their buying habits. How do they make purchasing decisions? What influences their decisions? By understanding your ideal customer's buying habits, you can tailor your marketing efforts to reach them at the right time and with the right message.

Understanding your ideal customer has several benefits. First, it allows you to create marketing messages that resonate with them and position yourself as the perfect solution to their needs. Second, it enables you to tailor your services to meet their specific requirements, which can lead to higher customer satisfaction. Third, it can help you differentiate yourself from your competitors and give you a competitive advantage.

The emotional reward of understanding your ideal customer is the ability to build strong relationships with them. By understanding their needs and challenges, you can provide them with the support and solutions they need to succeed. When you help your ideal customer achieve their goals, you not only build a loyal customer base, but you also derive a sense of fulfillment from making a positive impact on their lives.

In conclusion, understanding your ideal customer is essential for building a successful virtual assistant business. By identifying their demographics, psychographics, pain points, and buying habits, you can tailor your marketing efforts to reach them and position yourself as the perfect solution to their needs. The emotional reward of building strong relationships with your ideal customer and helping them achieve their goals is an added benefit that makes understanding your ideal customer all the more fulfilling.

# Creating a Professional Online Presence

In today's digital age, having a professional online presence is essential for any virtual assistant looking to attract clients and build a successful business. Your online presence is the first impression that potential clients will have of you, so it is important to make it a good one. In this chapter, we will explore the key elements of creating a professional online presence.

The first step in creating a professional online presence is to develop a strong personal brand. Your personal brand is the image that you project to the world, and it should reflect your values, skills, and expertise. A strong personal brand can help you stand out from the competition and position yourself as an expert in your field.

Next, you need to create a professional website. Your website is your virtual storefront, and it should be designed to attract and engage potential clients. Your website should be easy to navigate, visually appealing, and optimized for search engines. It should also provide clear and concise information about your services, your experience, and your expertise.

Another important element of creating a professional online presence is to be active on social media. Social media platforms such as LinkedIn, Twitter, and Facebook can help you reach a wider audience and connect with potential clients. You should post regularly on social media, share valuable content, and engage with your followers to build relationships and establish yourself as an expert in your field.

You should also create a portfolio of your work. Your portfolio should showcase your best work and demonstrate your expertise. It should include examples of projects that you have worked on, testimonials from satisfied clients, and any other relevant information that can help you attract potential clients.

In addition to these key elements, you should also ensure that your online presence is consistent and professional across all channels. This means using a consistent tone of voice, using professional photos, and ensuring that all of your online profiles are up-to-date and accurate.

Creating a professional online presence has several benefits. First, it can help you attract potential clients and build a strong customer base. Second, it can help you establish yourself as an expert in your field and differentiate yourself from the competition. Third, it can help you build relationships with potential clients and establish trust and credibility.

The emotional reward of creating a professional online presence is the ability to showcase your expertise and make a positive impact on the lives of your clients. By creating a strong personal brand, a professional website, a portfolio of your work, and a consistent online presence, you can position yourself as the perfect solution to your clients' needs and help them achieve their goals.

In conclusion, creating a professional online presence is essential for any virtual assistant looking to attract clients and build a successful business. By developing a strong personal brand, creating a professional website, being active on social media, creating a portfolio of your work, and ensuring that your online presence is consistent and professional, you can position yourself as an expert in your field and attract potential clients. The emotional reward of making a positive impact on the lives of your clients is an added benefit that makes creating a professional online presence all the more fulfilling.

# The Power of Social Media for Finding Clients

Social media has become an essential tool for virtual assistants looking to find clients and build a successful business. With billions of people using social media platforms such as Facebook, Instagram, Twitter, and LinkedIn, it is a powerful way to reach a wider audience and connect with potential clients. In this chapter, we will explore the key elements of using social media to find clients.

The first step in using social media to find clients is to identify the platforms that are most relevant to your target market. Different social media platforms attract different types of users, so it is important to choose the platforms that your ideal customer is most likely to use. For example, if you specialize in business services, LinkedIn may be the most relevant platform for you.

Once you have identified the platforms that are most relevant to your target market, you need to create a strong profile. Your profile should be professional, engaging, and reflective of your personal brand. It should provide clear and concise information about your services, your experience, and your expertise. You should also include a professional photo and a cover image that reflects your personal brand.

Next, you need to post regularly on social media. Your posts should be relevant, informative, and engaging. They should provide value to your followers and position you as an expert in your field. You should also use hashtags and other relevant keywords to make it easier for potential clients to find you.

Another important element of using social media to find clients is to engage with your followers. You should respond to comments and messages promptly, and engage in conversations with your followers. This can help you build relationships and establish trust and credibility with potential clients.

In addition to posting and engaging, you should also use social media advertising to reach a wider audience. Social media advertising allows you to target specific demographics, interests, and behaviors, which can help you reach the right people. You should also use retargeting ads to target people who have already shown an interest in your services.

Using social media to find clients has several benefits. First, it allows you to reach a wider audience and connect with potential clients from around the world. Second, it can help you establish yourself as an expert in your field and build trust and credibility with potential clients. Third, it can help you attract more clients and build a successful business.

The emotional reward of using social media to find clients is the ability to connect with people from around the world and make a positive impact on their lives. By providing value to your followers, engaging in conversations, and delivering quality services, you can build strong relationships with your clients and make a difference in their lives.

In conclusion, social media is a powerful tool for virtual assistants looking to find clients and build a successful business. By identifying the platforms that are most relevant to your target market, creating a strong profile, posting regularly, engaging with your followers, and using social media advertising, you can attract more clients and build a successful business. The emotional reward of connecting with people from around the world and making a positive impact on their lives is an added benefit that makes using social media all the more fulfilling.

# Building a Network of Referral Sources

One of the most effective ways for virtual assistants to find new clients is through word-of-mouth referrals. Referrals from satisfied clients or other professionals in your network can be a powerful way to attract new clients and build a successful business. In this chapter, we will explore the key elements of building a network of referral sources.

The first step in building a network of referral sources is to provide exceptional service to your existing clients. When you deliver quality work and provide exceptional customer service, your clients are more likely to refer you to others in their network. This is because they trust you and believe that you can provide the same level of service to their contacts.

Next, you need to actively seek out referrals from your existing clients. You can do this by asking for referrals directly, either in person or through email. You should also make it easy for your clients to refer you by providing them with referral cards or other promotional materials that they can pass along to others.

Another important element of building a network of referral sources is to connect with other professionals in your industry. This can include other virtual assistants, business coaches, marketing professionals, and other professionals who work with the same target market as you. By building relationships with these professionals, you can develop a network of trusted referral sources who can refer you to their clients and contacts.

It is also important to participate in networking events and online communities where you can connect with potential referral sources. This can include industry events, online forums, and social media groups. By participating in these events and communities, you can build relationships with other professionals and establish yourself as a credible and trustworthy resource.

Building a network of referral sources has several benefits. First, it can help you attract new clients and build a successful business. Referrals from satisfied clients and other professionals can be a powerful way to attract new business and build a strong customer base. Second, it can help you establish trust and credibility with potential clients. When someone refers you to a potential client, they are essentially vouching for your expertise and quality of work. Third, it can help you differentiate yourself from the competition. When you are referred by a trusted source, you are more likely to stand out from other virtual assistants who are competing for the same business.

The emotional reward of building a network of referral sources is the ability to make strong connections with other professionals and help your clients achieve their goals. By building relationships with other professionals and delivering quality work to your clients, you can make a positive impact on their lives and help them succeed.

In conclusion, building a network of referral sources is an essential element of building a successful virtual assistant business. By providing exceptional service to your existing clients, actively seeking out referrals, connecting with other professionals in your industry, and participating in networking events and online communities, you can attract more clients and build a successful business. The emotional reward of building strong connections and making a positive impact on the lives of your clients is an added benefit that makes building a network of referral sources all the more fulfilling.

# Creating a Strong Brand Identity

Creating a strong brand identity is essential for any virtual assistant looking to attract clients and build a successful business. Your brand identity is the image that you project to the world, and it should reflect your values, skills, and expertise. In this chapter, we will explore the key elements of creating a strong brand identity.

The first step in creating a strong brand identity is to define your brand values. Your brand values are the guiding principles that define your business and your approach to your work. Your brand values should be aligned with your personal values and should reflect the qualities that you want to be known for. Examples of brand values might include reliability, expertise, creativity, and integrity.

Next, you need to develop a brand voice. Your brand voice is the tone and style that you use in your marketing and communications. It should reflect your brand values and be consistent across all channels. For example, if your brand values include professionalism and expertise, your brand voice should be authoritative and informative.

Another important element of creating a strong brand identity is to develop a brand visual identity. Your brand visual identity includes elements such as your logo, color scheme, typography, and imagery. Your visual identity should be consistent across all channels, and it should reflect your brand values and brand voice.

It is also important to develop a brand personality. Your brand personality is the human characteristics that you assign to your brand. It can include elements such as humor, friendliness, or professionalism. By developing a brand personality, you can make your brand more relatable and engaging to your target market.

In addition to these key elements, it is also important to create a brand experience that reflects your brand identity. Your brand experience should be consistent across all touchpoints, from your website to your social media profiles to your customer service interactions. By delivering a consistent brand experience, you can build trust and credibility with your clients and position yourself as a reliable and trustworthy partner.

Creating a strong brand identity has several benefits. First, it can help you attract potential clients and build a strong customer base. Second, it can help you differentiate yourself from the competition and establish yourself as an expert in your field. Third, it can help you build trust and credibility with your clients, which can lead to higher customer satisfaction and retention.

The emotional reward of creating a strong brand identity is the ability to make a positive impact on the lives of your clients. By delivering a consistent brand experience and positioning yourself as a reliable and trustworthy partner, you can help your clients achieve their goals and make a positive impact on their lives.

In conclusion, creating a strong brand identity is essential for any virtual assistant looking to attract clients and build a successful business. By defining your brand values, developing a brand voice, creating a visual identity, developing a brand personality, and delivering a consistent brand experience, you can attract potential clients and build a strong customer base. The emotional reward of making a positive impact on the lives of your clients is an added benefit that makes creating a strong brand identity all the more fulfilling.

# Creating a Compelling Value Proposition

A value proposition is a statement that communicates the unique value that you offer to your clients. It is an essential element of your marketing strategy and can help you attract potential clients and differentiate yourself from the competition. In this chapter, we will explore the key elements of creating a compelling value proposition.

The first step in creating a compelling value proposition is to understand your target market. You need to know who your ideal customer is, what their needs and pain points are, and how you can help them achieve their goals. By understanding your target market, you can create a value proposition that resonates with them and addresses their specific needs.

Next, you need to identify your unique selling proposition (USP). Your USP is the thing that sets you apart from the competition and makes you stand out to your target market. It might be a specific skill or expertise, a unique approach to problem-solving, or a commitment to exceptional customer service.

Once you have identified your USP, you need to craft a value proposition that communicates the unique value that you offer to your clients. Your value proposition should be clear, concise, and focused on the benefits that you offer to your clients. It should answer the question, "Why should a potential customer choose you over the competition?"

Your value proposition should also be customer-focused. It should communicate the specific ways in which you can help your clients achieve their goals and solve their problems. By focusing on the customer and their needs, you can make your value proposition more compelling and relevant.

Another important element of creating a compelling value proposition is to back it up with evidence. This can include testimonials from satisfied clients, case studies that demonstrate your expertise, or statistics that show the impact that you have had on your clients' businesses.

Creating a compelling value proposition has several benefits. First, it can help you attract potential clients and differentiate yourself from the competition. By communicating the unique value that you offer, you can position yourself as the perfect solution to your clients' needs. Second, it can help you establish trust and credibility with potential clients. By providing evidence to back up your value proposition, you can demonstrate your expertise and track record of success. Third, it can help you increase customer satisfaction and retention. By focusing on the specific needs of your clients and delivering value that addresses those needs, you can build long-term relationships with your clients.

The emotional reward of creating a compelling value proposition is the ability to make a positive impact on the lives of your clients. By communicating the unique value that you offer and delivering exceptional service, you can help your clients achieve their goals and make a positive impact on their lives.

In conclusion, creating a compelling value proposition is essential for any virtual assistant looking to attract clients and build a successful business. By understanding your target market, identifying your USP, crafting a customer-focused value proposition, and backing it up with evidence, you can differentiate yourself from the competition and attract potential clients. The emotional reward of making a positive impact on the lives of your clients is an added benefit that makes creating a compelling value proposition all the more fulfilling.

# Creating a Portfolio of Work

A portfolio of work is an essential tool for any virtual assistant looking to attract clients and showcase their skills and expertise. It allows potential clients to see examples of your work and understand the value that you can offer to their business. In this chapter, we will explore the key elements of creating a portfolio of work.

The first step in creating a portfolio of work is to identify the types of work that you want to showcase. This might include samples of writing, social media posts, website design, or other projects that demonstrate your skills and expertise. It is important to choose examples that are relevant to your target market and highlight your unique value proposition.

Once you have identified the types of work that you want to showcase, you need to collect examples of your work. You can do this by asking previous clients for permission to use their work as examples, or by creating samples specifically for your portfolio. It is important to ensure that all examples are of high quality and showcase your skills and expertise.

Another important element of creating a portfolio of work is to organize your examples in a clear and compelling way. You can do this by creating a portfolio website, or by using other online tools such as Dropbox or Google Drive. Your portfolio should be easy to navigate and should include clear descriptions of each example, highlighting the skills and expertise that you demonstrated in each project.

In addition to showcasing your work, it is also important to include testimonials from satisfied clients. Testimonials can help to establish trust and credibility with potential clients, and demonstrate the value that you can offer to their business. You can also include case studies that demonstrate your expertise and the impact that you have had on your clients' businesses.

Creating a portfolio of work has several benefits. First, it can help you attract potential clients and differentiate yourself from the competition. By showcasing your skills and expertise, you can position yourself as the perfect solution to your clients' needs. Second, it can help you establish trust and credibility with potential clients. By including testimonials and case studies, you can demonstrate your track record of success and expertise. Third, it can help you increase customer satisfaction and retention. By showcasing the quality of your work and the value that you can offer to their business, you can build long-term relationships with your clients.

The emotional reward of creating a portfolio of work is the ability to make a positive impact on the lives of your clients. By showcasing your skills and expertise, and delivering exceptional work, you can help your clients achieve their goals and make a positive impact on their businesses.

In conclusion, creating a portfolio of work is an essential tool for any virtual assistant looking to attract clients and showcase their skills and expertise. By identifying the types of work that you want to showcase, collecting examples, organizing them in a clear and compelling way, and including testimonials and case studies, you can differentiate yourself from the competition and attract potential clients. The emotional reward of making a positive impact on the lives of your clients is an added benefit that makes creating a portfolio of work all the more fulfilling.

# Creating a Website That Converts Visitors into Clients

A website is an essential tool for any virtual assistant looking to attract clients and build a successful business. It is often the first point of contact that potential clients have with your business, and it can make a significant impact on their decision to work with you. In this chapter, we will explore the key elements of creating a website that converts visitors into clients.

The first step in creating a website that converts visitors into clients is to define your target market and value proposition. Your website should be designed to appeal to your target market and communicate the unique value that you offer to your clients. It should be clear, concise, and focused on the benefits that you offer to your clients.

Next, you need to create a compelling home page. Your home page is the first thing that potential clients will see when they visit your website, and it should make a strong impression. Your home page should be visually appealing, with clear and concise messaging that communicates the value that you offer to your clients.

Another important element of creating a website that converts visitors into clients is to include clear calls-to-action (CTAs). Your CTAs should be prominently displayed on your website and should encourage visitors to take action, such as filling out a contact form or scheduling a consultation.

It is also important to include social proof on your website. Social proof includes elements such as customer testimonials, case studies, and awards or recognition that you have received. By including social proof, you can build trust and credibility with potential clients and increase the likelihood that they will choose to work with you.

In addition to these key elements, it is also important to ensure that your website is user-friendly and easy to navigate. Your website should be optimized for mobile devices, as more and more people are using their smartphones and tablets to browse the internet. It should also be easy to navigate, with a clear and intuitive menu that directs visitors to the information that they are looking for.

Creating a website that converts visitors into clients has several benefits. First, it can help you attract potential clients and differentiate yourself from the competition. By communicating the unique value that you offer and including clear CTAs, you can encourage visitors to take action and work with you. Second, it can help you establish trust and credibility with potential clients. By including social proof, you can demonstrate your track record of success and expertise. Third, it can help you increase customer satisfaction and retention. By providing a user-friendly and engaging website, you can build long-term relationships with your clients.

The emotional reward of creating a website that converts visitors into clients is the ability to make a positive impact on the lives of your clients. By providing a website that communicates the unique value that you offer and encourages visitors to take action, you can help your clients achieve their goals and make a positive impact on their businesses.

In conclusion, creating a website that converts visitors into clients is an essential tool for any virtual assistant looking to attract clients and build a successful business. By defining your target market and value proposition, creating a compelling home page, including clear CTAs and social proof, and ensuring that your website is user-friendly and easy to navigate, you can differentiate yourself from the competition and attract potential clients. The emotional reward of making a positive impact on the lives of your clients is an added benefit that makes creating a website that converts visitors into clients all the more fulfilling.

# Building an Email List and Creating Effective Email Marketing Campaigns

Email marketing is a powerful tool for any virtual assistant looking to attract clients and build a successful business. By building an email list and creating effective email marketing campaigns, you can communicate with potential and existing clients, build relationships, and increase your business revenue. In this chapter, we will explore the key elements of building an email list and creating effective email marketing campaigns.

The first step in building an email list is to create a lead magnet. A lead magnet is an incentive that you offer to potential clients in exchange for their email address. It could be a free e-book, a checklist, a webinar, or any other resource that is valuable to your target market. Your lead magnet should be aligned with your value proposition and should provide a solution to a problem that your target market is facing.

Next, you need to create an opt-in form that allows potential clients to sign up for your email list. Your opt-in form should be prominently displayed on your website and should be easy to fill out. It should also clearly communicate the benefits of signing up for your email list, such as exclusive content or special offers.

Once you have built your email list, you need to create effective email marketing campaigns. The first step in creating effective email marketing campaigns is to segment your email list. Segmentation involves dividing your email list into groups based on specific criteria, such as location, interests, or behavior. By segmenting your email list, you can tailor your messages to the specific needs and interests of each group.

Another important element of creating effective email marketing campaigns is to create engaging and relevant content. Your emails should be focused on providing value to your subscribers, whether that means offering tips and advice, sharing industry news, or promoting your services. Your content should be relevant to your target market and should be consistent with your brand voice and values.

It is also important to pay attention to your email subject lines and design. Your subject line is the first thing that your subscribers will see, and it can make a significant impact on whether or not they open your email. Your design should be visually appealing and should make it easy for subscribers to read and engage with your content.

Finally, you need to track and analyze the results of your email marketing campaigns. This can include metrics such as open rates, click-through rates, and conversions. By tracking and analyzing your results, you can identify what is working and what is not, and make adjustments to improve the effectiveness of your campaigns.

Building an email list and creating effective email marketing campaigns has several benefits. First, it can help you attract potential clients and build relationships with existing clients. By providing valuable content and engaging with your subscribers, you can position yourself as an expert in your field and build trust and credibility. Second, it can help you increase customer satisfaction and retention. By providing personalized and relevant content, you can build long-term relationships with your clients.

The emotional reward of building an email list and creating effective email marketing campaigns is the ability to make a positive impact on the lives of your clients. By providing valuable content and engaging with your subscribers, you can help them achieve their goals and make a positive impact on their businesses.

In conclusion, building an email list and creating effective email marketing campaigns is an essential tool for any virtual assistant looking to attract clients and build a successful business. By creating a lead magnet and opt-in form, segmenting your email list, creating engaging and relevant content, paying attention to your subject lines and design, and tracking and analyzing your results, you can differentiate yourself from the competition and attract potential clients. The emotional reward of making a positive impact on the lives of your clients is an added benefit that makes building an email list and creating effective email marketing campaigns all the more fulfilling.

# Creating a Blog That Showcases Your Expertise

A blog is an excellent tool for any virtual assistant looking to attract clients and build a successful business. By creating a blog that showcases your expertise, you can provide valuable information to your target market, position yourself as an expert in your field, and increase your visibility online. In this chapter, we will explore the key elements of creating a blog that showcases your expertise.

The first step in creating a blog that showcases your expertise is to identify your target market and the topics that are relevant to them. Your blog should be focused on providing valuable information to your target market, whether that means offering tips and advice, sharing industry news, or discussing current trends.

Next, you need to create a content plan that includes a schedule for publishing blog posts. Your content plan should be aligned with your overall marketing strategy and should be consistent with your brand voice and values. It should also be focused on providing value to your target market and showcasing your expertise.

Another important element of creating a blog that showcases your expertise is to optimize your blog posts for search engines. This includes using keywords that are relevant to your target market, optimizing your headlines and subheadings, and using meta descriptions that entice potential readers to click through to your blog.

It is also important to create engaging and visually appealing blog posts. Your blog posts should be easy to read and understand, with clear and concise messaging. They should also include images, videos, or other visual elements that enhance the reader's experience and make your content more engaging.

Finally, you need to promote your blog posts on social media and other online channels. This can include sharing your blog posts on LinkedIn, Twitter, and other social media platforms, as well as including links to your blog in your email signature and other marketing materials.

Creating a blog that showcases your expertise has several benefits. First, it can help you attract potential clients and differentiate yourself from the competition. By providing valuable information to your target market, you can position yourself as an expert in your field and build trust and credibility. Second, it can help you increase customer satisfaction and retention. By providing consistent and valuable content, you can build long-term relationships with your clients.

The emotional reward of creating a blog that showcases your expertise is the ability to make a positive impact on the lives of your clients. By providing valuable information and insights, you can help your clients achieve their goals and make a positive impact on their businesses.

In conclusion, creating a blog that showcases your expertise is an essential tool for any virtual assistant looking to attract clients and build a successful business. By identifying your target market, creating a content plan, optimizing your blog posts for search engines, creating engaging and visually appealing blog posts, and promoting your blog on social media and other online channels, you can differentiate yourself from the competition and attract potential clients. The emotional reward of making a positive impact on the lives of your clients is an added benefit that makes creating a blog that showcases your expertise all the more fulfilling.

# Building a Presence on Freelancer Platforms

Freelancer platforms are an excellent way for virtual assistants to find clients and build a successful business. By building a presence on freelancer platforms, you can connect with potential clients, showcase your skills and experience, and increase your visibility online. In this chapter, we will explore the key elements of building a presence on freelancer platforms.

The first step in building a presence on freelancer platforms is to identify the platforms that are relevant to your target market and the services that you offer. There are many freelancer platforms available, including Upwork, Freelancer.com, and Fiverr. Each platform has its own unique features and requirements, so it is important to do your research and choose the platforms that are the best fit for your business.

Next, you need to create a profile on each platform that you have chosen. Your profile should be focused on showcasing your skills and experience, and should be aligned with your brand voice and values. It should also include a professional profile picture and a well-written bio that communicates your unique value proposition.

Another important element of building a presence on freelancer platforms is to create a portfolio of work. Your portfolio should include examples of your best work and should be focused on demonstrating your skills and expertise. It should also be easy to navigate and visually appealing, with clear and concise messaging.

It is also important to optimize your profile for search engines. This includes using keywords that are relevant to your target market, optimizing your headline and summary, and using meta descriptions that entice potential clients to click through to your profile.

Finally, you need to actively participate on each platform that you have chosen. This includes submitting proposals for relevant projects, responding to messages and inquiries in a timely manner, and delivering high-quality work that meets or exceeds your clients' expectations.

Building a presence on freelancer platforms has several benefits. First, it can help you attract potential clients and differentiate yourself from the competition. By creating a professional and engaging profile, showcasing your skills and experience, and delivering high-quality work, you can build trust and credibility with your clients. Second, it can help you increase customer satisfaction and retention. By providing excellent service and delivering high-quality work, you can build long-term relationships with your clients.

The emotional reward of building a presence on freelancer platforms is the ability to make a positive impact on the lives of your clients. By providing excellent service and delivering high-quality work, you can help your clients achieve their goals and make a positive impact on their businesses.

In conclusion, building a presence on freelancer platforms is an essential tool for any virtual assistant looking to attract clients and build a successful business. By identifying the platforms that are relevant to your target market and the services that you offer, creating a professional profile and portfolio of work, optimizing your profile for search engines, and actively participating on each platform, you can differentiate yourself from the competition and attract potential clients. The emotional reward of making a positive impact on the lives of your clients is an added benefit that makes building a presence on freelancer platforms all the more fulfilling.

# Creating Partnerships with Other Virtual Assistants

Creating partnerships with other virtual assistants is an excellent way to find clients and build a successful business. By partnering with other virtual assistants, you can tap into their networks, share resources and knowledge, and collaborate on projects. In this chapter, we will explore the key elements of creating partnerships with other virtual assistants.

The first step in creating partnerships with other virtual assistants is to identify the virtual assistants that are relevant to your target market and the services that you offer. This could include virtual assistants who offer complementary services, virtual assistants who work with similar types of clients, or virtual assistants who are located in the same geographic area as you.

Next, you need to reach out to the virtual assistants that you have identified and initiate a conversation. This could involve sending an email, a LinkedIn message, or a direct message on social media. Your message should be focused on introducing yourself, explaining why you are interested in partnering with them, and suggesting a time to chat further.

Another important element of creating partnerships with other virtual assistants is to establish clear and open communication. This includes setting expectations around communication channels, frequency, and response times. It also involves being transparent about your availability, workload, and any potential conflicts of interest.

It is also important to establish clear boundaries and guidelines around how you will work together. This could include defining roles and responsibilities, agreeing on pricing and payment terms, and outlining how you will handle any disagreements or issues that arise.

Finally, you need to actively collaborate with the virtual assistants that you have partnered with. This could involve sharing leads and referrals, working together on joint projects, or exchanging knowledge and resources. It is important to be proactive and to communicate regularly to ensure that your partnership is successful.

Creating partnerships with other virtual assistants has several benefits. First, it can help you attract potential clients and expand your network. By partnering with other virtual assistants, you can tap into their networks and gain exposure to potential clients that you may not have otherwise had access to. Second, it can help you build relationships and collaborate with other professionals in your field. This can lead to valuable knowledge sharing and resource sharing opportunities.

The emotional reward of creating partnerships with other virtual assistants is the ability to make a positive impact on the lives of your clients. By collaborating with other professionals, you can provide your clients with a wider range of services and expertise, which can help them achieve their goals and make a positive impact on their businesses.

In conclusion, creating partnerships with other virtual assistants is an essential tool for any virtual assistant looking to find clients and build a successful business. By identifying relevant virtual assistants, establishing clear and open communication, setting boundaries and guidelines, and actively collaborating, you can differentiate yourself from the competition and attract potential clients. The emotional reward of making a positive impact on the lives of your clients is an added benefit that makes creating partnerships with other virtual assistants all the more fulfilling.

# Creating a Pricing Strategy That Works for You and Your Clients

Creating a pricing strategy that works for you and your clients is an essential element of building a successful virtual assistant business. Your pricing strategy should be aligned with your value proposition and your target market, and should allow you to make a profit while still being competitive in the marketplace. In this chapter, we will explore the key elements of creating a pricing strategy that works for you and your clients.

The first step in creating a pricing strategy is to identify your value proposition and your target market. Your value proposition is what sets you apart from the competition and should be reflected in your pricing. Your target market is the group of people who are most likely to need and value your services, and should be considered when setting your prices.

Next, you need to determine your costs and overhead. This includes calculating the time and resources that you need to complete each project, as well as any overhead expenses such as software subscriptions, marketing costs, and other business expenses. This will help you determine the minimum amount that you need to charge in order to make a profit.

Another important element of creating a pricing strategy is to research your competition. This involves researching what other virtual assistants are charging for similar services, and comparing your pricing to theirs. This will help you determine whether your prices are competitive in the marketplace, and whether you need to adjust your prices to be more competitive.

It is also important to consider the perceived value of your services. This includes factors such as your experience, expertise, and the quality of your work. By emphasizing the value that you provide, you can justify higher prices and differentiate yourself from the competition.

Finally, you need to communicate your pricing clearly to your clients. This includes being transparent about your pricing structure and the services that you provide, and providing clear and detailed invoices that outline the work that you have done. It is also important to be flexible and willing to negotiate with clients, especially for long-term projects or repeat clients.

Creating a pricing strategy that works for you and your clients has several benefits. First, it can help you attract potential clients and differentiate yourself from the competition. By offering competitive pricing and emphasizing the value that you provide, you can position yourself as a trusted and reliable partner for your clients. Second, it can help you increase customer satisfaction and retention. By providing transparent and detailed invoices, and by being flexible and willing to negotiate, you can build long-term relationships with your clients.

The emotional reward of creating a pricing strategy that works for you and your clients is the ability to make a positive impact on the lives of your clients. By providing high-quality services at a fair price, you can help your clients achieve their goals and make a positive impact on their businesses.

In conclusion, creating a pricing strategy that works for you and your clients is an essential tool for any virtual assistant looking to build a successful business. By identifying your value proposition and target market, determining your costs and overhead, researching your competition, emphasizing the value that you provide, and communicating your pricing clearly to your clients, you can differentiate yourself from the competition and attract potential clients. The emotional reward of making a positive impact on the lives of your clients is an added benefit that makes creating a pricing strategy all the more fulfilling.

# Understanding the Importance of Customer Service

Customer service is an essential element of any successful business, and as a virtual assistant, it is especially important to provide exceptional customer service to your clients. By understanding the importance of customer service, you can build long-term relationships with your clients, increase customer satisfaction and retention, and differentiate yourself from the competition. In this chapter, we will explore the key elements of understanding the importance of customer service.

The first step in understanding the importance of customer service is to recognize that your clients are the lifeblood of your business. Without satisfied and loyal clients, your business will struggle to succeed. Providing exceptional customer service is a key way to attract and retain clients, and to build a positive reputation in the marketplace.

Next, you need to identify the key elements of exceptional customer service. This includes being responsive to your clients' needs and concerns, providing high-quality work that meets or exceeds their expectations, and communicating regularly and transparently. It also involves being proactive in identifying and addressing issues before they become problems, and being flexible and accommodating to your clients' needs and schedules.

Another important element of exceptional customer service is to establish clear and consistent communication channels. This includes determining the best way to communicate with each client, whether it is through email, phone, or video chat. It also involves establishing clear expectations around response times, availability, and any potential communication barriers such as time zone differences.

It is also important to create a culture of customer service within your business. This involves emphasizing the importance of customer service to your team members, and providing training and resources to help them deliver exceptional customer service. It also involves soliciting feedback from your clients and using that feedback to continually improve your services and customer experience.

Finally, you need to recognize the emotional rewards of providing exceptional customer service. By making a positive impact on the lives of your clients, you can build long-term relationships with them and become a trusted and valued partner. You can also take pride in knowing that you are helping your clients achieve their goals and make a positive impact on their businesses.

In conclusion, understanding the importance of customer service is an essential element of building a successful virtual assistant business. By recognizing the importance of your clients, identifying the key elements of exceptional customer service, establishing clear communication channels, creating a culture of customer service, and recognizing the emotional rewards of providing exceptional customer service, you can differentiate yourself from the competition and attract and retain loyal clients. The emotional reward of making a positive impact on the lives of your clients is an added benefit that makes providing exceptional customer service all the more fulfilling.

# Creating a System for Onboarding New Clients

Onboarding new clients is an important element of building a successful virtual assistant business. By creating a system for onboarding new clients, you can streamline the process, ensure that your clients are satisfied with your services, and set the stage for a successful long-term relationship. In this chapter, we will explore the key elements of creating a system for onboarding new clients.

The first step in creating a system for onboarding new clients is to establish clear expectations and goals. This includes understanding your client's needs and goals, and communicating your own goals and expectations for the project. It also involves setting clear timelines, milestones, and deliverables, and establishing a process for communicating progress and updates.

Next, you need to create a welcome packet or onboarding guide that outlines your services, processes, and expectations. This packet should include information about your services, your pricing and payment policies, and any relevant terms and conditions. It should also include an overview of the onboarding process, including the steps that will be taken, the timeline for completion, and any deliverables that the client can expect.

Another important element of onboarding new clients is to establish clear communication channels. This includes determining the best way to communicate with each client, whether it is through email, phone, or video chat. It also involves establishing clear expectations around response times, availability, and any potential communication barriers such as time zone differences.

It is also important to establish a process for gathering and sharing information. This includes creating templates for client intake forms, project briefs, and other relevant documents. It also involves establishing a process for sharing files and collaborating on projects.

Finally, you need to follow up with your clients after the onboarding process is complete. This includes soliciting feedback on the onboarding process and the services that you provided, and using that feedback to continually improve your services and customer experience. It also involves checking in with your clients periodically to ensure that they are satisfied with your services and to identify any potential issues or opportunities for improvement.

Creating a system for onboarding new clients has several benefits. First, it can help you attract potential clients and differentiate yourself from the competition. By providing a streamlined and professional onboarding experience, you can build trust and credibility with your clients. Second, it can help you increase customer satisfaction and retention. By establishing clear expectations and goals, and by communicating regularly and transparently, you can build long-term relationships with your clients.

The emotional reward of creating a system for onboarding new clients is the ability to make a positive impact on the lives of your clients. By providing a professional and welcoming onboarding experience, you can help your clients achieve their goals and make a positive impact on their businesses.

In conclusion, creating a system for onboarding new clients is an essential tool for any virtual assistant looking to build a successful business. By establishing clear expectations and goals, creating a welcome packet or onboarding guide, establishing clear communication channels, creating templates for gathering and sharing information, and following up with your clients after the onboarding process is complete, you can differentiate yourself from the competition and attract and retain loyal clients. The emotional reward of making a positive impact on the lives of your clients is an added benefit that makes creating a system for onboarding new clients all the more fulfilling.

# Building Long-Term Relationships with Clients

Building long-term relationships with clients is an essential element of building a successful virtual assistant business. By focusing on the needs and goals of your clients, communicating regularly and transparently, and providing exceptional customer service, you can build trust and credibility with your clients and establish yourself as a valued and trusted partner. In this chapter, we will explore the key elements of building long-term relationships with clients.

The first step in building long-term relationships with clients is to understand their needs and goals. This involves listening to their feedback, asking questions, and identifying opportunities to add value to their businesses. It also involves being proactive in identifying and addressing issues or challenges that they may be facing.

Next, you need to establish clear and consistent communication channels. This includes determining the best way to communicate with each client, whether it is through email, phone, or video chat. It also involves establishing clear expectations around response times, availability, and any potential communication barriers such as time zone differences.

Another important element of building long-term relationships with clients is to provide exceptional customer service. This includes being responsive to your clients' needs and concerns, providing high-quality work that meets or exceeds their expectations, and being flexible and accommodating to their needs and schedules. It also involves being proactive in identifying and addressing issues before they become problems, and being transparent and honest in your communications.

It is also important to establish trust and credibility with your clients. This includes being reliable and consistent in your work, and being transparent about your processes, pricing, and policies. It also involves demonstrating expertise and knowledge in your field, and being willing to share that knowledge with your clients.

Finally, you need to recognize the emotional rewards of building long-term relationships with clients. By making a positive impact on the lives of your clients, you can build a sense of satisfaction and fulfillment in your work. You can also take pride in knowing that you are helping your clients achieve their goals and make a positive impact on their businesses.

Building long-term relationships with clients has several benefits. First, it can help you attract potential clients and differentiate yourself from the competition. By establishing yourself as a trusted and reliable partner, you can build a positive reputation in the marketplace. Second, it can help you increase customer satisfaction and retention. By providing exceptional customer service and building trust and credibility with your clients, you can build long-term relationships that result in repeat business and referrals.

In conclusion, building long-term relationships with clients is an essential element of building a successful virtual assistant business. By understanding their needs and goals, establishing clear and consistent communication channels, providing exceptional customer service, building trust and credibility, and recognizing the emotional rewards of your work, you can differentiate yourself from the competition and attract and retain loyal clients. The emotional reward of making a positive impact on the lives of your clients is an added benefit that makes building long-term relationships with clients all the more fulfilling.

# Identifying Opportunities for Upselling and Cross-Selling

As a virtual assistant, identifying opportunities for upselling and cross-selling can be an effective way to increase your revenue and build stronger relationships with your clients. By understanding their needs and goals, and identifying opportunities to provide additional services or products, you can add value to their businesses and increase their satisfaction with your services. In this chapter, we will explore the key elements of identifying opportunities for upselling and cross-selling.

The first step in identifying opportunities for upselling and cross-selling is to understand your clients' needs and goals. This involves listening to their feedback, asking questions, and identifying opportunities to add value to their businesses. It also involves understanding their business models and identifying areas where you can provide additional support or services.

Next, you need to identify the types of services or products that you can offer as part of an upsell or cross-sell. This may include complementary services or products that align with your existing services, or new services or products that address a specific need or pain point that your clients are experiencing.

Another important element of identifying opportunities for upselling and cross-selling is to communicate the value of these additional services or products to your clients. This includes explaining how they can benefit from these additional offerings, and how they can help them achieve their goals and improve their businesses.

It is also important to establish clear pricing and payment policies for these additional services or products. This includes communicating the pricing and payment terms upfront, and ensuring that your clients understand the costs and benefits associated with these offerings.

Finally, you need to recognize the emotional rewards of identifying opportunities for upselling and cross-selling. By making a positive impact on the lives of your clients, you can build a sense of satisfaction and fulfillment in your work. You can also take pride in knowing that you are helping your clients achieve their goals and make a positive impact on their businesses.

Identifying opportunities for upselling and cross-selling has several benefits. First, it can help you increase your revenue and profitability. By offering additional services or products to your existing clients, you can generate more revenue without having to spend additional time or resources on marketing and sales. Second, it can help you build stronger relationships with your clients. By demonstrating your expertise and knowledge, and by offering additional value to their businesses, you can build trust and credibility with your clients.

In conclusion, identifying opportunities for upselling and cross-selling is an effective way to increase your revenue and build stronger relationships with your clients as a virtual assistant. By understanding their needs and goals, identifying the types of services or products that you can offer, communicating the value of these offerings, establishing clear pricing and payment policies, and recognizing the emotional rewards of your work, you can differentiate yourself from the competition and attract and retain loyal clients. The emotional reward of making a positive impact on the lives of your clients is an added benefit that makes identifying opportunities for upselling and cross-selling all the more fulfilling.

# Creating a System for Tracking and Managing Your Clients

As a virtual assistant, it is essential to have a system for tracking and managing your clients. By having a clear process for managing your clients, you can ensure that you are providing high-quality service, meeting their needs and goals, and building long-term relationships. In this chapter, we will explore the key elements of creating a system for tracking and managing your clients.

The first step in creating a system for tracking and managing your clients is to establish a centralized system for storing and organizing client information. This may include a CRM (customer relationship management) system or a simple spreadsheet that includes client contact information, project details, timelines, and other relevant information.

Next, you need to establish a process for tracking client interactions and communications. This includes logging all phone calls, emails, and other communication with your clients. It also involves setting reminders and follow-up tasks to ensure that you are responding to your clients' needs and concerns in a timely and effective manner.

Another important element of creating a system for tracking and managing your clients is to establish a process for tracking project progress and deadlines. This includes setting clear project milestones and deadlines, and tracking progress against these milestones. It also involves communicating progress updates to your clients on a regular basis, and being transparent about any potential delays or issues that may arise.

It is also important to establish a process for managing client feedback and concerns. This includes being responsive to your clients' feedback and concerns, and addressing any issues or challenges that they may be facing. It also involves being proactive in identifying and addressing potential issues before they become problems, and being transparent and honest in your communications.

Finally, you need to recognize the emotional rewards of creating a system for tracking and managing your clients. By providing high-quality service, meeting your clients' needs and goals, and building long-term relationships, you can build a sense of satisfaction and fulfillment in your work. You can also take pride in knowing that you are helping your clients achieve their goals and make a positive impact on their businesses.

Creating a system for tracking and managing your clients has several benefits. First, it can help you provide high-quality service and build long-term relationships with your clients. By establishing clear processes and systems for managing your clients, you can ensure that you are providing a consistent and reliable service. Second, it can help you increase your productivity and efficiency. By streamlining your client management processes, you can free up more time to focus on delivering high-quality work.

In conclusion, creating a system for tracking and managing your clients is an essential tool for any virtual assistant looking to build a successful business. By establishing a centralized system for storing and organizing client information, tracking client interactions and communications, tracking project progress and deadlines, managing client feedback and concerns, and recognizing the emotional rewards of your work, you can differentiate yourself from the competition and attract and retain loyal clients. The emotional reward of making a positive impact on the lives of your clients is an added benefit that makes creating a system for tracking and managing your clients all the more fulfilling.

# Scaling Your Virtual Assistant Business for Long-Term Success

As a virtual assistant, scaling your business is essential for long-term success. By increasing your revenue, expanding your client base, and developing new services or products, you can build a sustainable and profitable business that meets your goals and provides value to your clients. In this chapter, we will explore the key elements of scaling your virtual assistant business for long-term success.

The first step in scaling your virtual assistant business is to establish a clear vision and goals for your business. This involves identifying your strengths and weaknesses, understanding your market and competition, and defining your unique value proposition. It also involves setting clear revenue and growth goals, and developing a plan for achieving these goals.

Next, you need to identify opportunities for expansion and growth. This may include expanding your services or products, developing new niches or markets, or increasing your marketing and sales efforts. It also involves investing in technology and tools that can help you automate and streamline your business processes.

Another important element of scaling your virtual assistant business is to establish a strong team and infrastructure. This includes hiring and training additional staff or contractors, establishing clear processes and workflows, and investing in technology and tools that can help you manage and track your team's work.

It is also important to establish clear financial and operational metrics for measuring and managing your business. This includes tracking revenue, expenses, profit margins, and other key performance indicators. It also involves establishing clear policies and procedures for managing cash flow, invoicing, and billing.

Finally, you need to recognize the emotional rewards of scaling your virtual assistant business. By building a sustainable and profitable business, you can achieve financial independence, provide value to your clients, and make a positive impact on your industry and community. You can also take pride in knowing that you are building a legacy that can benefit future generations.

Scaling your virtual assistant business has several benefits. First, it can help you increase your revenue and profitability, and achieve financial independence. Second, it can help you expand your impact and influence, and make a positive impact on your industry and community. Third, it can help you build a sustainable and profitable business that provides value to your clients and team members.

In conclusion, scaling your virtual assistant business is essential for long-term success. By establishing a clear vision and goals, identifying opportunities for expansion and growth, establishing a strong team and infrastructure, tracking financial and operational metrics, and recognizing the emotional rewards of your work, you can build a sustainable and profitable business that meets your goals and provides value to your clients. The emotional reward of making a positive impact on the lives of your clients and team members is an added benefit that makes scaling your virtual assistant business all the more fulfilling.

# Conclusion

As we come to the end of this book, we hope that you have gained valuable insights into how to find clients as a virtual assistant. From defining your niche and target market, to building a professional online presence, to creating a system for tracking and managing your clients, to scaling your business for long-term success, we have covered a range of topics that are essential for building a successful virtual assistant business.

One of the key themes that has emerged throughout this book is the importance of understanding your clients and their needs. By listening to their feedback, asking questions, and identifying opportunities to add value to their businesses, you can differentiate yourself from the competition and build long-term relationships that are based on trust and mutual benefit.

Another important theme is the power of technology and tools in streamlining your business processes and increasing your efficiency. By investing in technology and tools that can help you automate and streamline your work, you can free up more time to focus on delivering high-quality service and building strong relationships with your clients.

But perhaps the most important theme is the emotional reward of being a virtual assistant. By making a positive impact on the lives of your clients, you can build a sense of satisfaction and fulfillment in your work. You can also take pride in knowing that you are helping your clients achieve their goals and make a positive impact on their businesses.

In conclusion, being a virtual assistant is a rewarding and fulfilling career that offers a range of benefits and opportunities for growth and success. By understanding your clients, investing in technology and tools, and recognizing the emotional rewards of your work, you can build a successful and sustainable business that meets your goals and provides value to your clients. We hope that this book has provided you with the knowledge and insights that you need to find clients as a virtual assistant and build a successful career in this exciting and dynamic field.

Thank You for Reading!

We want to extend a heartfelt thank you for taking the time to read this book on how to find clients as a virtual assistant. We hope that you have found it informative, engaging, and inspiring, and that it has provided you with valuable insights into building a successful virtual assistant business.

We would greatly appreciate it if you could take a few moments to leave a positive review of this book on the platform where you purchased it. Your review will help other readers discover this book and benefit from the knowledge and insights that it contains.

Once again, thank you for reading, and we wish you all the best in your journey as a virtual assistant!

www.ingramcontent.com/pod-product-compliance
Lightning Source LLC
Chambersburg PA
CBHW071046220526
45467CB00004B/1699